Rock Guitar Playing
Grade Three

Compiled by
Tony Skinner and Merv Young
on behalf of
Registry Of Guitar Tutors
www.RGT.org

Printed and bound in Great Britain

A CIP record for this publication is available from the British Library
ISBN: 978-1-905908-33-2

Published by Registry Publications

Registry Mews, Wilton Rd, Bexhill, Sussex, TN40 1HY

Cover photo by Andreas Gradin/Fotolia. Design by JAK Images.

Compiled by

v.20111111

Contents

Page

Introduction

This book is part of a progressive series of ten handbooks designed for rock guitarists who wish to develop their playing and obtain a qualification. Although the primary intention of these handbooks is to prepare candidates for the Registry Of Guitar Tutors (RGT) rock guitar exams, the series provides a comprehensive structure that will help develop the abilities of any guitarist interested in rock music, whether or not intending to take an exam.

Those preparing for an exam should use this handbook in conjunction with the *Syllabus for Rock Guitar Playing* and the *Rock Guitar Exam Information Booklet* – both freely downloadable from the RGT website: **www.RGT.org**

Exam Outline

There are three components to this exam, each of which is briefly outlined below:

❶ **Prepared Performances.** The performance, along to backing tracks, of special arrangements of two classic rock pieces.

❷ **Improvisation.** This is in two parts: firstly, improvisation of a lead guitar solo over a previously unseen chord progression, followed by improvisation of a rhythm guitar part over the same chord progression. Playing will be to a backing track provided by the examiner.

❸ **Aural Assessment.** This will consist of a 'Rhythm Test' (repeating the rhythm of a riff), a 'Pitch Test' (reproducing a riff on the guitar) and a 'Chord Recognition Test' (identifying a chord).

Mark Scheme

The maximum marks available for each component are:

- Prepared Performances: 60 marks (30 marks per piece).
- Improvisation: 30 marks.
- Aural Assessment: 10 marks.

To pass the exam candidates need a total of 65 marks. Candidates achieving 75 marks will be awarded a Merit certificate, or a Distinction certificate for 85 marks or above.

Tuning

For exam purposes guitars should be tuned to Standard Concert Pitch (A=440Hz). The use of an electronic tuner or other tuning aid is permitted. The examiner will not assist with tuning other than to, upon request, offer an E or A note to tune to.

Notation

Within this handbook, scales and chords are illustrated in three formats: traditional notation, tablature and fretboxes – thereby ensuring that there is no doubt as to how to play each scale or chord. Each of these methods of notation is explained below.

Traditional Notation: Each line, and space between lines, represents a different note. Leger lines are used to extend the stave for low or high notes. For scales, fret and string numbers are printed below the notation: fret-hand fingering is shown with the numbers 1 2 3 4, with 0 indicating an open string; string numbers are shown in a circle. The example below shows a two-octave G major scale.

Tablature: Horizontal lines represent the strings (with the top line being the high E string). The numbers on the string lines refer to the frets. 0 on a line means play that string open (unfretted). The example below means play at the second fret on the third string.

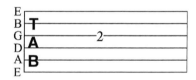

Fretboxes: Vertical lines represent the strings – with the line furthest to the right representing the high E string. Horizontal lines represent the frets. The numbers on the lines show the recommended fingering. 1 represents the index finger, 2 = the long middle finger, 3 = the ring finger, 4 = the little finger. The example below means play with the second finger at the second fret on the G string.

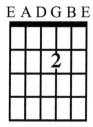

Fingering Options

The fret-hand fingerings that have been chosen are those that are most likely to be effective for the widest range of players at this level. However, there are a variety of alternative fingerings that could be used, and any systematic and effective fingerings that produce a good musical result will be acceptable; there is no requirement to use the exact fingerings shown within this handbook.

Exam Entry

An exam entry form is provided at the rear of this handbook. This is the only valid entry form for the RGT rock guitar playing exams.

Please note that if the entry form is detached and lost, it will not be replaced under any circumstances and the candidate will be required to obtain a replacement handbook to obtain another entry form.

The entry form includes a unique entry code to enable online entry via the RGT website **www.RGT.org**

About Registry of Guitar Tutors (RGT)

- RGT was established in 1992 and is the world's largest organisation of guitar educators.

- RGT organises exams in a wide range of guitar styles, from beginner to professional Diploma level, in numerous countries around the world.

- RGT exams are operated in partnership with London College of Music Exams, which was founded in 1887 and is one of the world's most respected music examination boards.

- The qualifications are awarded and certificated by the University of West London and, from Grade One onwards, are accredited by Ofqual and have been placed on the Qualifications and Credit Framework. From Grade Six onwards, RGT exams attract UCAS points which can be used towards university entrance.

For more information about RGT visit www.RGT.org

Prepared Performances

Candidates should choose and perform TWO of the following classic rock pieces:

❶ All Right Now – Free

❷ Paranoid – Black Sabbath

❸ Pinball Wizard – The Who

Obtaining the notation and audio

These pieces have been specifically arranged for the RGT Grade Three Rock Guitar Playing exam and are notated in TAB and standard notation in the publication *Graded Guitar Songs – 9 Rock Classics for Beginning Level Guitarists**. This also includes a CD that features each track being performed in full, as well as a backing track for each piece for the candidate to perform with during the exam. These tracks have been specially recorded to suit RGT exam requirements.

*For copyright ownership reasons, the notation and audio tracks for these pieces cannot be included in this RGT grade handbook. However, they are all included in the book *Graded Guitar Songs – 9 Rock Classics for Beginning Level Guitarists*, which is available from *www.BooksForGuitar.com* or can be ordered from most music stores. *Graded Guitar Songs – 9 Rock Classics for Beginning Level Guitarists* contains all performance pieces that are required for the RGT rock guitar playing exams Grades One, Two and Three.

Exam format

Candidates' performances should be accurate reproductions of the specially arranged versions of the pieces as notated and recorded in the book *Graded Guitar Songs – 9 Rock Classics for Beginning Level Guitarists*. Alternative fingerings and playing positions to those shown in the book can be adopted if preferred, provided the overall musical result is not altered from the recorded version.

Performances do not need to be from memory; candidates should remember to bring their book to the exam should they wish to refer to the notation.

The performances should be played along to the specially recorded backing tracks supplied on the CD that is included with the book *Graded Guitar Songs – 9 Rock Classics for Beginning Level Guitarists*. Alternative recordings of the pieces will not be accepted as backing tracks. There is no need to bring your CD to the exam, as the examiner will provide the necessary backing tracks during the exam.

Prior to the performance commencing, candidates will be allowed a brief 'soundcheck' so that they can choose their sound and volume level. Candidates can use either a clean or a distorted guitar sound for their performance of these tracks, and can bring their own distortion or other effects units to the exam *providing that they can set them up promptly and unaided.*

In order to achieve a high mark in this section of the exam, performances should be fully accurate and very confidently presented. Timing, clarity and technical control should be totally secure throughout, and some expressive qualities (such as varying the dynamics of the performance) should be displayed.

Performance Tips

All Right Now – Free

The RGT arrangement of this piece is in the original key of A major. The four bar riff that features in the intro and verse sections starts with an open position A major chord. In order to change smoothly and fluently onto the D/A chord that follows, it is recommended that you play the A major chord using the first finger of your fretting hand; this keeps your second and third fingers free to fret the remaining notes needed for the D/A chord. (The chord symbol D/A indicates that this is a 'slash chord' in which you should play an inversion of D major with A as the bass note.)

In the third bar, as well as the subtle chord change that occurs, there is an added challenge of reproducing the rhythm accurately. Care needs to be taken to ensure that only the B, G and D strings are sounded when strumming this pattern. The rhythm itself is also quite tricky, so listen to the recorded track carefully to ensure that you are familiar with how this section should sound.

The chorus uses mainly power chords played on the D and G strings. In some places, rests (i.e. silences) often occur between chords, so where rests are marked in the notation make sure you either bring your picking hand against the strings to stop them from ringing out or release the pressure with the fretting hand to create the same result. In some bars, power chords are required to ring out across more than a whole bar; count the timing on these sustained power chords carefully to ensure that all the notes ring out for the correct period of time.

The instrumental section in this arrangement is an abridged and slightly simplified version of the guitar solo that features on the original version of the track, although it does include a number of the main elements and phrases from the original solo. Consider carefully which finger to use for the slide up from fret 3 to fret 10 in bars 27 and 28 as you will need to be ready for the faster phrase that follows it. These faster, hammer-on phrases in bars 29 and 31 will need careful practice to ensure the rhythm is smooth and even – listen to the recorded track for confirmation of how the rhythm should sound here. Towards the end of the instrumental there are a few whole tone bends from fret 12 of the B string; take care with all of these to ensure that the string is being bent up to the correct pitch each time.

Paranoid – Black Sabbath

The RGT arrangement of this piece is in the original key of E minor. The eight bar introduction to this track features a series of hammer-ons. The notation and recorded track will need to be followed carefully here to ensure that the rhythm is performed accurately. The first three hammer-ons are played as quickly as possible, whereas the hammer-ons in bar 2 have an even eighth note rhythm. There is also an added challenge in the first bar where the rhythm is syncopated (i.e. some notes are played across the beat). Listen to the recorded track carefully to ensure you are familiar with how this should sound.

Power chords then dominate the track with a fast, even rhythm being required to provide energy and momentum to the music. The abbreviation 'P.M.' in the notation indicates the use of 'palm muting'. Bring the side or edge of your picking hand gently against the bass strings at the bridge. You should still be able to strum the bass strings, although the strumming movement will be restricted a little. Particularly when deployed with a distorted guitar sound, this will give you the classic "chugging" rhythm of this track. Follow the notation and practise carefully to ensure that you start and stop this palm-muting technique in the correct places.

Although the bridge section only contains two different power chords, each one ringing out for two bars, take care to count the beats in this section carefully. Each chord should ring out for eight beats in total so count these off and then confidently strike the next chord.

Pinball Wizard – The Who

The RGT arrangement of this piece moves through the same keys as the original artist's recording; commencing in B minor, then predominantly B major for the remainder of the track until a modulation to a D major key centre for the ending.

The three note chords that feature in the intro should each be allowed to ring out for the full four beats each, before switching to the next one. The rhythm then becomes more complex in the final three bars of the intro, so listen to the recorded track and follow the notation carefully here.

The rhythm part that is notated for the second intro and the verse is performed on an acoustic guitar on the original artist's recording, although our recorded track features an electric guitar. Keep your strumming as light and smooth as possible here to ensure the even flow of the 16th notes that are notated – don't grip the pick too tightly as this may cause the rhythm to falter. The first and seventh chords in each bar feature an accent mark (>) above the notation. On these accented beats try to slightly emphasise the chord by strumming it a little harder – but don't overdo it or you'll lose the flow of the rhythm. The biggest challenge in this section is the stamina required to maintain the rhythm across all of the chord changes. Practise it slowly at first and focus on one chord at a time before trying to play the entire verse all the way through.

The riff that comes in at bar 20 is an instrumental break in the track, so try to strum the chords here with some energy, although not at the expense of the notated rhythm. Take care to follow the rests (i.e. silences) that occur here and ensure that the strings are as silent as possible during these chord changes.

The penultimate bar of the chorus contains a variation of the D chord that produces a Dsus4 chord by moving the note on fret 7 of the B string up to fret 8. In order to ensure this chord transition sounds as smooth as possible, try to keep the rest of the D chord in place as you move your little finger up one fret.

Improvisation

The candidate will be shown a previously unseen chord chart in $\frac{4}{4}$ time. This will consist of an 8-bar chord progression, which will be played five times non-stop (via a pre-recorded backing track).

- During the first verse, the candidate should just listen to the track while reading the chord chart.

- A 4-beat count-in will be given and then during the next two verses, the candidate should improvise a lead guitar solo.

- A 4-beat count-in will be given and then during the last two verses, the candidate should improvise a rhythm guitar part.

- The backing track will end with the first chord of the progression played once.

Candidates will be given a short time to study the chord chart and will then be allowed a brief 'soundcheck' with the track prior to the performance commencing, so that they can choose their sound and volume level. Candidates can bring their own distortion or other effects units to the exam *providing that* they can set them up promptly and unaided.

The backing track will include drums, bass and rhythm guitar for the first three verses, but in the last two verses the recorded rhythm guitar part will be omitted so that the candidate can perform their own rhythm guitar part.

The rhythm guitar part that is recorded on the backing track gives an indication of the standard of rhythm playing that is expected for this section of the exam. Candidates do not need to reproduce exactly the rhythm part that is recorded on the backing track. They should, however, strive to perform a rhythm part that is stylistically appropriate and with a "feel" that is in keeping with the backing track. Part of the assessment here will be centred on the candidate's ability to listen and then perform an appropriate rhythm part.

The range of chords that may appear in the backing tracks for this grade is detailed on following pages. As the chord progression will be previously unseen by the candidate, the candidate will need to be fully familiar with all the chords listed for the grade in order to be properly prepared for the chord progressions that will occur in the exam. At this grade, chords are expected to be fingered as barré chords or power chords – however, the occasional use of open position chords, where this enhances the musical performance, is acceptable. Each chord progression will consist of chords grouped together into appropriate keys. Several examples of the type of chord progression that will occur at this grade are provided at the end of this chapter.

In order to improvise a lead guitar solo accurately and effectively, candidates will need to learn a range of appropriate scales upon which to base their improvisation. The first chord in the progression will be the key chord and will, therefore, indicate the scale that would generally be best to use for improvising a lead solo; the recommended scales that could be used to improvise over the chord progressions at this grade are provided later in this chapter. Although other scale options and improvisation approaches exist, it is highly recommended that candidates acquire a thorough knowledge of the scales listed for the grade, as these will provide a core foundation for improvisation at the appropriate level of technical development. However, providing they produce an effective musical result, other appropriate scale choices or improvisation approaches will also be acceptable.

The examiner will not provide any advice regarding identifying the key or guidance on which scale to use.

⬇ Volume Changes

When playing your lead guitar improvisation, your volume will need to be loud enough to be clearly heard over the accompaniment. When switching to rhythm playing, during the improvisation section of the exam, you will almost certainly need to quickly adjust the volume of your guitar, as the settings you have used for single-note lead playing may be too loud and could overpower the accompaniment if used when strumming chords during the rhythm playing.

There are numerous ways this volume change could be made; at this grade, one of the following methods would be the most straightforward:

• Turn down the volume control on your guitar.

• Use the pick-up selector on your guitar to switch to a pick-up with a lower output, or (if your guitar has more than one volume control) to a pick-up that you have pre-adjusted to a lower volume setting.

• If you are using your own distortion/overdrive unit for lead playing, turn this off and use a quieter clean sound for rhythm playing.

Prior to the exam, it is important to practise and become adept at making this volume change – as during the exam it will need to be done quickly and smoothly during the last bar of the lead guitar section, so that you are ready to begin the rhythm playing section in time.

Chords

Here is the range of chords that may occur in the chord progressions for this grade.

•	Major barré chords:	G, A, B, C, D, E
•	Minor barré chords:	Gm, Am, Bm, Cm, Dm, Em
•	Fifth (power) chords:	G5, A5, B5, C5, D5, E5

G major

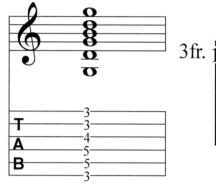 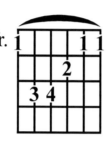

A major

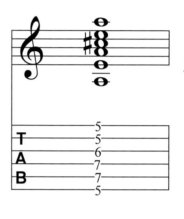 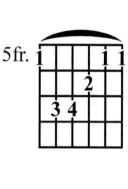

B major

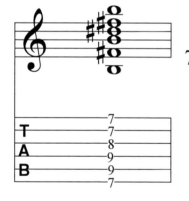 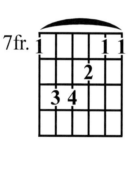

C major

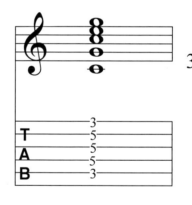 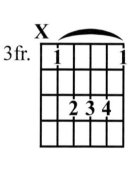

D major

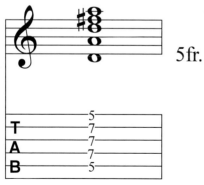 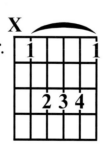

E major

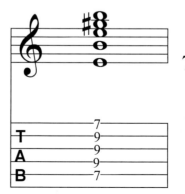 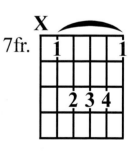

G minor

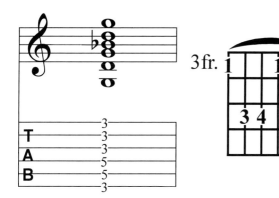

A minor

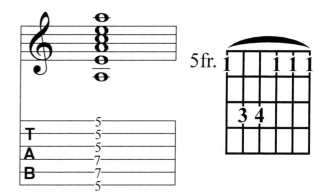

B minor

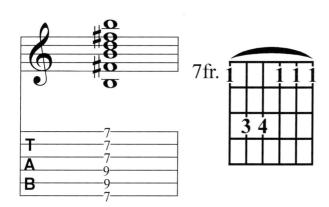

C minor

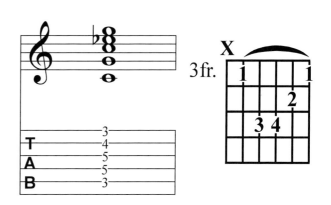

D minor

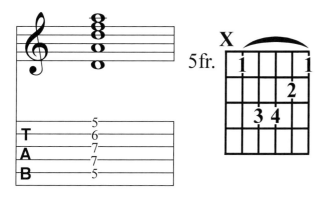

E minor

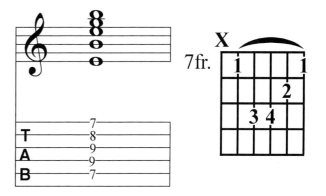

G5

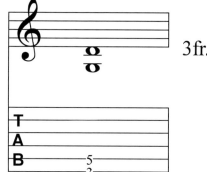

A5

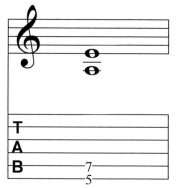

B5

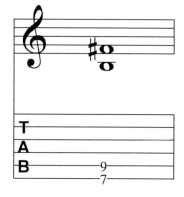

C5

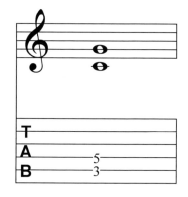

D5

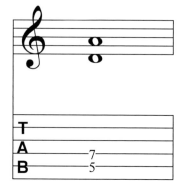

E5

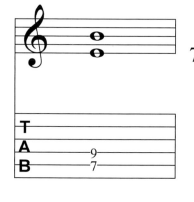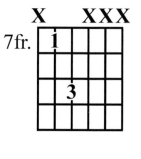

Scales

Here is the range of scales recommended for use during the lead guitar improvisation section of the exam at this grade.

Scale:	Range of chords that may be included in the exam progression:
G major	G Am Bm C D Em
A blues	A5 C5 D5 E5 G5
B pentatonic minor	Bm D Em G A
C pentatonic major	C Dm Em G Am
D natural minor	Dm Gm Am C

Improvisation using two-octave fretted scales is expected at this grade.

G major scale – 2 octaves
G A B C D E F# G

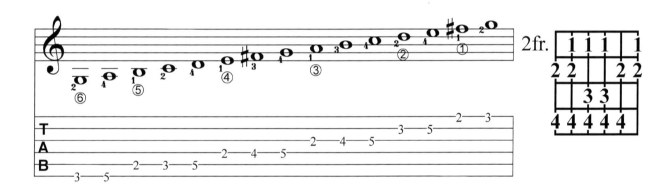

A blues scale – 2 octaves
A C D Eb E G A

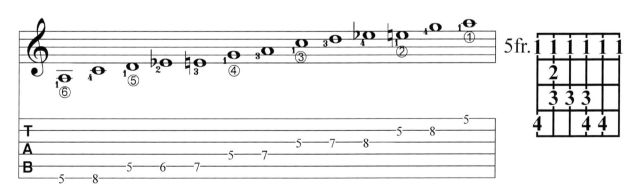

B pentatonic minor scale – 2 octaves
B D E F# A B

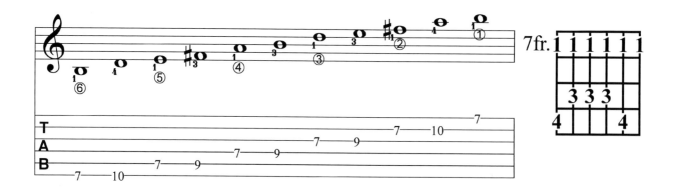

C pentatonic major scale – 2 octaves
C D E G A C

D natural minor scale – 2 octaves
D E F G A Bb C

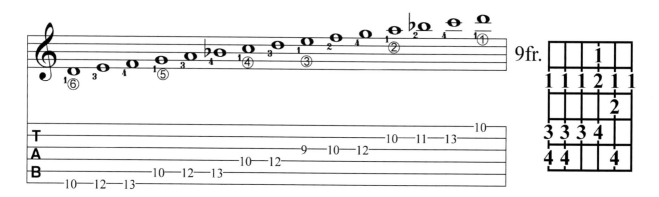

Performance Advice

In order to attain high marks in this section of the exam, the performance needs to be fully accurate and confident in execution, with a high level of clarity and fluency appropriate to the grade. There should be evidence of stylistic interpretation, inventiveness and creativity.

As the improvised rhythm playing will be performed over a recorded backing track, the emphasis will be on developing key performance skills such as rhythmic security and fluency. The use of rhythm guitar techniques such as palm muting and 'ghost strums' is encouraged where this would appropriately enhance the musical performance, however the use of these techniques at this grade is not expected to be extensive. Dynamic markings are not included on the chord charts, to enable candidates to focus on their own rhythmic and dynamic interpretation.

The improvised lead solo should be accurate in terms of note selection and timing in relation to the accompaniment. There should be evidence of melodic phrasing and shaping. The use of specialist techniques such as string bending, vibrato, slides and slurs (i.e. hammer-ons and pull-offs) should be used to enhance the musical performance, and a basic grasp of at least some of these techniques is expected to be demonstrated at this grade, when musically appropriate.

Performance Tips

➢ Try to use the short period of study time, when you're first shown the chord chart, as effectively as possible by looking through the chart to ensure you are confident with the chords that occur and with your choice of scale.

➢ During the first verse of the backing track, follow the chord chart carefully and get ready to start your lead guitar improvisation after the 4 beat count-in.

➢ Listen carefully to the backing track throughout the performance to ensure that your lead and rhythm playing is rhythmically secure; try to make your playing relate to what the bass and drums are playing.

➢ Keep an awareness of where you are in the chord chart, so that the 4 beat count-in to commence your rhythm playing doesn't take you by surprise – as the examiner will not re-start the backing track once it is underway.

➢ During the lead improvising listen carefully to what you are playing to make it sound as musically effective as you can and try to create musical phrases. Use techniques such as string bends, vibrato and slurs to enhance the expressiveness of your lead solo.

➢ Prior to exam day, when preparing for this section of the exam ensure that you are completely confident knowing, and changing between, all the chords that may occur; during the exam itself you can then focus on playing the chords as confidently and musically as possible.

➢ The example chord charts that are provided overleaf give an indication of what to expect in the exam, but these are not the actual charts that will be given. In preparing for this section of the exam you are advised to download all these example backing tracks to ensure you are comfortable with improvising both lead and rhythm parts over the range of tempos and styles indicated by these examples.

Example Chord Progressions

The following are examples of the type of chord progression candidates may be presented with in this section of the exam. Please note that the scale suggestions shown above each progression will NOT appear in the charts presented during the exam.

Improvisation Chart Example 1

G major scale could be used to improvise over this progression.

| $\frac{4}{4}$ G | | G | Bm | Bm | |
| Am | | C | D | Em | |

Improvisation Chart Example 2

A blues scale could be used to improvise over this progression.

| $\frac{4}{4}$ A5 | | A5 | C5 | G5 | |
| A5 | | C5 | E5 | E5 | |

Improvisation Chart Example 3

B pentatonic minor scale could be used to improvise over this progression.

| $\frac{4}{4}$ Bm | | D | Em | Em | |
| Bm | | G | A | A | |

Improvisation Chart Example 4

C pentatonic major scale could be used to improvise over this progression.

| $\frac{4}{4}$ C | C | Em | Am |

| C | C | Dm | G ‖

Improvisation Chart Example 5

D natural minor scale could be used to improvise over this progression.

| $\frac{4}{4}$ Dm | Gm | Dm | Am |

| Gm | Gm | C | C ‖

It is important to note that the sample chord progressions provided above are supplied purely to provide examples of the *type* of chord progression that may occur in the exam. These examples are NOT the actual chord progressions that candidates will be given in the exam.

Aural Assessment

Candidates' aural abilities will be assessed via a series of three aural tests:
• Rhythm test • Pitch test • Chord recognition test.

Rhythm Test

A riff is played three times via a recording. During the third playing the candidate is required to clap along with the exact *rhythm* of the riff.

At this grade, the riff will be two bars in length. The time signature will be $^4_4$. Note durations will not be shorter than eighth notes (quavers). Rests, ties and dotted notes may be included.

Examples of the *type* of riffs that will occur at this grade are shown below, with the rhythm to be clapped notated below the tab.

Pitch Test

The riff from the rhythm test is played two further times with a click track. A gap is left after each playing, so that the candidate can practice the riff. Then, after a one-bar count-in, the candidate is required to play along with a click track, accurately reproducing the riff on the guitar.

At this grade, the range of scales from which the riff will be derived is limited to those listed in the improvisation section of this handbook, i.e. G major, A blues, B pentatonic minor, C pentatonic major and D natural minor. The riff will start on the keynote. The examiner will state which scale the riff is taken from.

Below are some examples of the *type* of riffs that will occur at this grade in the rhythm and pitch tests.

Example 1 (from G major scale)

Example 2 (from A blues scale)

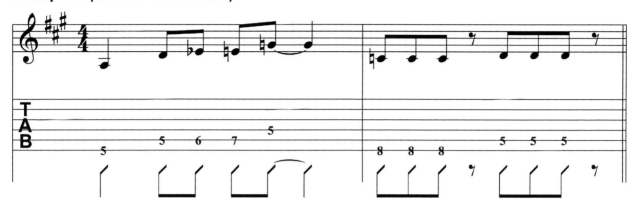

Example 3 (from B pentatonic minor scale)

Example 4 (from C pentatonic major scale)

Example 5 (from D natural minor scale)

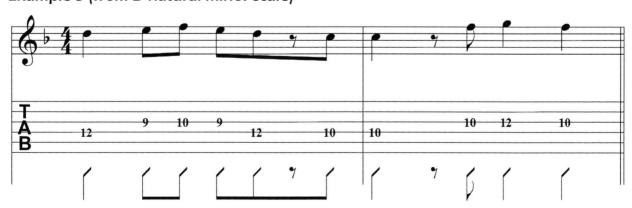

Chord Recognition Test

This test involves identifying the penultimate chord within a very short chord progression. The progression will be either in the key of G major or D major. It will start and end on the key chord and contain just one other chord – this will be either the IV chord (subdominant) or V chord (dominant) of the key, i.e. either C or D in the key of G major, or G or A in the key of D major; it is this chord that the candidate will be asked to identify.

The key will be stated and the progression will be played twice, before the candidate is required to answer. The candidate must not use the guitar to aid their answer.

Below are some examples of the *type* of chord progressions that will occur at this grade in the chord recognition tests.

Example 1

$\frac{4}{4}$ G | D   G   ‖

Example 2

$\frac{4}{4}$ G | C   G   ‖

Example 3

$\frac{4}{4}$ D | A   D   ‖

Example 4

$\frac{4}{4}$ D | G   D   ‖

✪Tip
In examples 1 and 3 the movement from the penultimate (V) chord to the final (I) chord creates a strong ending known as a 'perfect (or V-I) cadence'.
In examples 2 and 4 the movement from the penultimate (IV) chord to the final (I) chord creates a weaker, more subtle, ending known as a 'plagal (or IV-I) cadence'.
You will not be asked use these cadence names in the exam, but practising them and getting used to the sound of these cadences will help you recognise these chord movements.

It is important to note that the example tests provided above are supplied purely to provide examples of the *type* of test that may occur in the exam.

The Specialists in Guitar Education

RGT ®
Registry of Guitar Tutors

Exam Entry Form
Rock Guitar Grade ③

ONLINE ENTRY – AVAILABLE FOR UK CANDIDATES ONLY

For **UK candidates**, entries and payments can be made online at www.RGT.org, using the entry code below. You will be able to pay the entry fee by credit or debit card at a secure payment page on the website.

Your unique and confidential exam entry code is:

RC-8775-AN

Keep this unique code confidential, as it can only be used once. Once you have entered online, you should sign this form overleaf. **You must bring this signed form to your exam and hand it to the examiner in order to be admitted to the exam room.**

If NOT entering online, please complete BOTH sides of this form and return to the address overleaf.

SESSION (Spring/Summer/Winter): SUMMER   YEAR: 2013

Dates/times NOT available: _____

Note: Only name *specific* dates (and times on those dates) when it would be *absolutely impossible* for you to attend due to important prior commitments (such as pre-booked overseas travel) which cannot be cancelled. We will then endeavour to avoid scheduling an exam session in your area on those dates. In fairness to all other candidates in your area, **only list dates on which it would be impossible for you to attend.** An entry form that blocks out unreasonable periods may be returned. (Exams may be held on any day of the week including, but not exclusively, weekends. Exams may be held within or outside of the school term.)

Candidate Details: *Please write as clearly as possible using BLOCK CAPITALS*

Candidate Name (as to appear on certificate): _____

Address: _____

_____ Postcode: _____

Tel. No. (day): _____ (mobile): _____

IMPORTANT: Take care to write your email address below as clearly as possible, as your exam entry acknowledgement and your exam appointment details will be sent to this email address. Only provide an email address that is in regular monitored use.

Email:_____
Where an email address is provided your exam correspondence will be sent by email only, and not by post. This will ensure your exam correspondence will reach you sooner.

Teacher Details *(if applicable)*

Teacher Name (as to appear on certificate): PAUL ANDREWS

RGT Tutor Code (if applicable): PA2740

Address: 11 BLUEFIELD   SINGLETON   ASHFORD

_____ Postcode: TN23 5HW

Tel. No. (day): 01233 634 382   (mobile): 07984 726 413

Email: PAUL@ASHFORD GUITAR LESSONS.COM

RGT Rock Guitar Official Entry Form

- Completion of this entry form is an agreement to comply with the current syllabus requirements and conditions of entry published at www.RGT.org. Where candidates are entered for exams by a teacher, parent or guardian that person hereby takes responsibility that the candidate is entered in accordance with the current syllabus requirements and conditions of entry.

- If you are being taught by an *RGT registered* tutor, please hand this completed form to your tutor and request him/her to administer the entry on your behalf.

- For candidates with special needs, a letter giving details should be attached.

Exam Fee: £ _49.00_   Late Entry Fee (if applicable): £_____

Total amount submitted: £_____

Cheques or postal orders should be made payable to Registry of Guitar Tutors.

Details of conditions of entry, entry deadlines and exam fees are obtainable from the RGT website: www.RGT.org

Once an entry has been accepted, entry fees cannot be refunded.

CANDIDATE INFORMATION (UK Candidates only)

In order to meet our obligations in monitoring the implementation of equal opportunities policies, UK candidates are required to supply the information requested below. The information provided will in no way whatsoever influence the marks awarded during the exam.

Date of birth: _____ Age: _____ Gender – please circle: male / female

Ethnicity (please enter 2 digit code from chart below): _____ Signed: _____

ETHNIC ORIGIN CLASSIFICATIONS (If you prefer not to say, write '17' in the space above.)

White: **01 British**   **02 Irish**   **03 Other white background**

Mixed: **04 White & black Caribbean**   **05 White & black African**   **06 White & Asian**   **07 Other mixed background**

Asian or Asian British: **08 Indian**   **09 Pakistani**   **10 Bangladeshi**   **11 Other Asian background**

Black or Black British: **12 Caribbean**   **13 African**   **14 Other black background**

Chinese or Other Ethnic Group: **15 Chinese**   **16 Other**   **17 Prefer not to say**

I understand and accept the current syllabus regulations and conditions of entry for this exam as specified on the RGT website.

Signed by candidate (if aged 18 or over) _____ Date _____

If candidate is under 18, this form should be signed by a parent/guardian/teacher (circle which applies):

Signed _____ Name_____ Date_____

UK ENTRIES

See overleaf for details of how to enter online OR return this form to:
Registry of Guitar Tutors, Registry Mews, 11 to 13 Wilton Road, Bexhill-on-Sea, E. Sussex, TN40 1HY
(If you have submitted your entry online do NOT post this form, instead you need to sign it above and hand it to the examiner on the day of your exam.)
To contact the RGT office telephone 01424 222222 or Email office@RGT.org

NON-UK ENTRIES

To locate the address within your country that entry forms should be sent to, and to view exam fees in your currency, visit the RGT website **www.RGT.org** and navigate to the 'RGT Worldwide' section.